The Bottomland

The Bottomland

Poems by Harry Humes

THE UNIVERSITY OF ARKANSAS PRESS

FAYETTEVILLE 1995

Library of Congress Cataloging-in-Publication Data

Humes, Harry.
     The bottomland / Harry Humes.
        p.   cm.
     ISBN 1-55728-377-X (alk. paper).—ISBN 1-55728-380-X (pbk. : alk.
paper)
     1. Coal mines and mining—Pennsylvania—Poetry. 2. Family—
Pennsylvania—Poetry.   I. Title.
PS3558.U444B68 1995
811'.54—dc20   94-43871
                                                              CIP

Jacket/cover art *Pennsylvania Coal Town* by Edward Hopper courtesy
of The Butler Institute of American Art, Youngstown, Ohio.

For Nancy and my daughters, Leah and Rachel,
and for my brothers, Bill and Ed

Acknowledgments

Grateful acknowledgment is made to the editors of the following journals in which these poems first appeared: *Chester H. Jones Anthology:* "The Bottomland"; *Georgia Review:* "Showing a Friend My Town," "The Other End"; *Gettysburg Review:* "Two Beautiful Young Women," "The Grand Canyon"; *Heatherstone Press:* "Pennsylvania Coal Town," "Deep Water Swimming Lesson"; *Kansas Quarterly:* "Mustard Plaster"; *Kayak:* "The Names of Your Return"; *New Letters:* "Beach Tent"; *Poetry Northwest:* "Deer," "Hand Dancing," "Bear Jam," "My Father's Hands," "My Mother Ate Hill Dirt," "Fox," "Mine Settlement," "Dust," "Photograph of Three Young Women on a Spill Bank," "Vultures," "Dead Hawk," "The Mink"; *Quarterly West:* "Yonko"; *Shenandoah:* "Yellow Flowers," "The Last Woods Bison," "The Snow Boat," "The Comet"; *Sundog:* "The Cough"; *Verse:* "The Lime Kings"; *West Branch:* "My Wife Vanishes in a Field of Sunflowers," "Stealing Coal"; and *Yankee:* "The Last Day of August," "Migration."

I gratefully acknowledge the National Endowment for the Arts and the Pennsylvania Council of the Arts for their extremely generous help while I was working on this book. I would also like to thank Kutztown University and the Professional Development Committee of the Pennsylvania State System of Higher Education for a grant during the summer of 1993.

Additionally, I would like to thank those who looked at these poems in one stage or another and offered support and help: Fred Chappell, Dabney Stuart, Larry Holland, Frank Allen, Nancy Humes, Miller Williams, and the readers for the University of Arkansas Press.

In a different form, "The Cough" won the 1993 World's Greatest Short Short Story Competition.

Contents

The Names of Your Return   *1*

Showing a Friend My Town   *2*

Hand Dancing   *3*

My Father Made Bamboo Fly Rods   *5*

Mine Settlement   *7*

Pennsylvania Coal Town   *8*

Mustard Plaster   *10*

Dust   *12*

The Cough   *14*

The Other End   *16*

Migraine   *18*

Deep Water Swimming Lesson   *20*

The Comet   *22*

My Mother Ate Hill Dirt   *24*

Yonko   *26*

Stealing Coal   *28*

My Father's Hands   *29*

The Grand Canyon   *30*

Vultures   *32*

Fox   *34*

Deer   *35*

The Mink   *36*

Bear Jam   *37*

Two Beautiful Young Women   *39*

My Wife Vanishes in a Field of Sunflowers   *40*

A Small Lovely Place   *43*

Yellow Flowers   *44*

Beach Tent   *45*

The Bottomland   *47*

The Last Day of August   *49*

Migration   *51*

Dead Hawk   *52*

My Daughter Wakes in the Fog   *54*

The Snow Boat   *56*

The Last Woods Bison   *58*

The Lime Kings   *59*

Photograph of Three Young Women on a Spill Bank   *61*

The Names of Your Return

Drink horehound hot from the fire
if you are poisoned by your stepmother.
—folk tale

If you enter a warm room and ordinary light
gathers like white powder in all the corners,
if you walk down a street or through the old orchard
and have to stop for balance near buildings or burrow,
if you dream of each breath like a dark bird near your lips,
if you go out at noon and rub snow on your face and neck,
if your eyes burn and begin to see by two and three,
then surely one afternoon as you lie on you damp pallet
thinking of Argentina, you will notice your hands
clammy as dungeon walls, will touch your coarse hair,
your temple, nose, chest, dry knot of belly,

and know at last, at last, that after the house is sleeping
you must go to the garden of wonders and build a fire
and sit before the pot of dark leaves and think of the mother
of birches, mother of pure water, mother of blood,
mother of first light when you must take the hot juice
to your lips, throat, feeling the world come into balance again,
feeling your veins and lungs swelling with musk,
you must go on speaking the names of your return,
Seed of Borus, Bull's Blood, Herb of Mercury, Eye of the Star.

Showing a Friend My Town

These are the switchbacks off the ridge,
the shack where an old man froze one winter.
This is the swamp where each spring small frogs
float up to the low branches of white birches.
This is the alley, the telephone pole
where a father put up backboard and rim.
These are explosions, sirens, cries from dirt cellars.
These are bats and nighthawks, this the old railbed
to the mine, these the lace curtains that caught
a Sunday afternoon breeze, here are basement steps,
the door with its broken latch to the backyard,
the path up to the shadows beneath the laurels.
These are mothers leaning in good evening weather
across porches, their voices like white sheets
almost dry on the line. These are windowsills
coated with dust from trucks up and down High Road,
water streaming from tailgates, blast of air horns.
These are tomato plants growing in coal ash,
this the double mock orange bush, this the sage,
this the fox tail nailed to the pigeon coop.
This is the empty chair beneath the maple.

Hand Dancing

Suddenly I am up on my hands,
moving off between okra and beets,
corn dust drifting over my ankles and wrists.
The world has not been this way for years,
so I look for arrowheads, for the knife
I lost one summer. I move past onions
and Chinese radishes to the woodpile
where I rest, my hips relaxed,
legs easy against dry logs.
I pick up a leaf, a cicada shell,
watch the sun over the smokehouse.
Then I am off again, along the stream
where the mallards had their nest,
where the muskrat preens, then dives
when a stick snaps beneath my fingers.
I grow reckless, do a few spins,
a step or two my father taught me
all one January. From my pockets
fall coins, notebook, the small knife.
Doors and windows rattle and open,
cars slow down. I do a one-hander and wave.

Children begin to laugh. Voices gather
down by the picnic tables.
Then through the evening, flashlights.
I know what I have to do,
a few final turns, a small shift of focus
as my feet arc slowly down
through hyssop and jimson weed.
My cat comes out of nowhere and curls
against my legs. I rub its ears, its belly,
I tell the men I saw no one
up on his hands waving at the children,
that I am looking for red mushrooms,
for the wasp that lays its eggs
in the bellies of toads.
They nod, then move off across alfalfa
and winter wheat, their lights blurring,
voices smaller and smaller in the breeze.
Then back up I go, humming one of the old hymns,
my cat walking between my bruised hands,
both of us jaunty, content with the ground,
the way back through the shadows.

4

My Father Made Bamboo Fly Rods

After he came home from his mine,
after potato soup and hot black tea,
down he'd go into the back cellar,
culms of bamboo stacked in the corners
and hanging from the ceiling.
He'd take one in his hands,
checking for water stains, scuffs, scars,
running his fingers over the nodes.
Then with a knife and a rubber mallet,
he'd split the culm into strips,
his hands bleeding from the glass-sharp edges.
Months of evenings down there,
late summer into fall, fall into winter,
straightening the strips over a flame,
planing and tapering, gluing and wrapping.
One morning, it would be on the kitchen table,
six coats of varnish, red silk wrappings,
guides and ferrules shining.
Three rods a year, each one with
Stillwater written low on the butt piece.
When he put one into our hands,

it trembled through the cork handle
and seemed to want to fly off.
He'd take it down to the garden to test cast,
his arm hardly moving, the rod bending
behind him, then arcing forward,
line unwinding from a narrow loop,
almost invisible against the sky, and my father
telling us that bamboo was a grass,
and that the first bamboo rod makers
also made violins. Casting to one spot,
then another, as if trout
were working under peonies and sage,
as if he were writing something
there about his life.

Mine Settlement

Overnight, windows stuck fast,
doors would not close and hung half-opened
on bedrooms, cellar steps, furnace room.
The whole house shifted, went off plumb.
The Bible leaned off its shelf, water spilled
from saucers beneath my mother's African violets.
We walked with one foot lower, while my father
worked along the east foundation, setting up
the half dozen heavy jacks he raised slowly,
one turn at a time. Three days it took
for doors and windows to click shut,
another to lay in new concrete supports,
then the jacks were wound down, the house creaking
and shuddering. For a week we walked gently,
almost whispered to each other. We remembered
the woman hanging clothes who vanished
into the earth. No one slammed a door.
My father rolled a marble over the kitchen linoleum,
all of us happy when it did not roll back.
Nor did we name the abandoned tunnels beneath us,
their rotting timbers, drip of acid water and gas
dissolving the edges of what we most believed.

Pennsylvania Coal Town

after Edward Hopper

The man slumps a bit over his rake
and stares levelly between two houses.
Morning or evening sun slants through
to his white shirt and socks, the fern
in its sculpted urn, a toy wagon
with its handle low to the ground.
What has he seen or heard?
Something has let go, developed a crack,
or shifted no louder than a breath.
Windows are tightly curtained or dark.
Concrete steps lead to doors in shadows.
There is no sky. Behind him the lawn
drops steeply to the sidewalk bricks.
It is a green that no summer ever made.
No one else is there. Not a bakery truck.
No children playing ring-a-levio.
Maybe it is only his wife beating carpets
on a clothesline out back. Or a wren
with a pale grub in its beak.
It is all weighted with absence.
Not even there if you blink too often.

It might all be chalk.

You can feel powder on your lips.

That scraggly grass like a sputtered-out fuse—

nothing can be done with it.

Mine acid and smoke have burned it underneath.

The whole sorrow is balanced on his rake.

Mustard Plaster

Runny nose, hot forehead, no appetite,
and by late afternoon my cough worse,
a wheezing deep in my lungs,
ratcheting up through my throat.

After supper, my mother boiled water,
and spooned mustard powder into it.

I lay in the middle bedroom
dreading the moment she dipped
a cloth into the hot mix,
wrung it out and spread it over my chest,
then closed my pajama top over it,
smiling, patting me on the head.

All night it burned layer by layer
into my thin chest.
On and off I woke, afraid to touch
those soggy, yellow things weighing me down.
I thought morning would never come,
and the last plaster never peeled off,

that my mother would never place
her cool powdered wrist on my forehead,
and say, *There, there,*
that's much better.
And I never free of the mustard's fire,
whether cured or purified.

Dust

By late summer it hid the edges of things.
Ropes were strung along sidewalks—
church ropes, school ropes, work ropes,
ropes to the doctor and store,
ropes past big-headed Charles,
who groaned from his porch on Main Street,
baseball ropes, girlfriend ropes,
everything gray as the towels
our mother wedged against windows and doors
and over the radio's tubes. Ropes breaking
or tied by boys to a maple's high branch,
ropes shaking with the whistle and hiss of trains.
Before we slept our mother tied
blue work handkerchiefs over our mouths.
Then, just when we had the hang of dust,
all of us moving easily, friendly,
waiting our turn at intersections,
just when our hands were grooved and sure,
came first a tightness to the air,
a few drops, some wind, then the rain
slowly filling ravines and mine holes,

spilling into town, over the white crosses
of the American Legion Memorial,
flooding gutters, storm sewers, the creek
rising along its riprap. We watched
from attic windows, heard it against roofs,
along foundations, dissolving, clearing the air,
watched our fathers' cars take shape,
pigeon coops and dog pens come back,
green rocking chairs, movie marquee,
all of us shy, turning this way and that,
getting a new grip on each other.

The Cough

Our young father walked Ash Alley whistling
"Rescue the Perishing," but already he carried
mine tunnels home in his black-streaked breath.
It was like first sleet against an attic window.
My mother would look at him, her lips a line
of impatience and fear. *Your lungs will soon be stone,* she said.
It's good money, Dorse. It's the only money.

Some of the miners who stopped at our house
to see my father had tongues like fish
that stuck out between words.
Gray-faced, shoulders bony,
they all seemed about to cave in.
My mother would leave the room,
her lips thinner than ever, but the cough
followed her across the linoleum, down cellar steps,
hunkered close when she planted sage and primrose.

The cough was like a child.
It was always hungry. It demanded attention.
It woke us up at odd times and sat in the good chair by the
    window.

In winter, it trailed behind my father

like a peacock feather on a woman's hat.

One summer he told us we were on a planet going nowhere
fast.

He made a model he called an orrery, and showed us how the
heavens worked.

The center was bright and hung there like one of my mother's
peony blossoms.

That there's what pushes it, he said. *And that's what made the coal.*

We looked at him and nodded,

but we had our own ideas about what made it go.

We could hear it behind the least little thing.

The Other End

Even when my sister began coughing blood,
she would walk three blocks
to the drugstore phone booth,
and dial the boys who used to roar
past our house on Indian motorcycles.
The boys in their duck's ass haircuts
and tight pants, the boys she'd
go night swimming with at the Bricky,
the boys my father threatened, cursed, and ran off.
My sister talking into the phone
as if twenty years had not gone by,
her hazel eyes still sparkling,
her fingers making curlicues on the door's glass,
shaking out her thin hair as she talked
to some stranger at the other end.
When the druggist finally called us on his phone,
one of us would walk downtown for her
and knock softly on the booth.
She might have drifted off into sleep,
a line of spittle on her lips,
the receiver slipped from her grip,

or she might smile sweetly, shyly,
as if the evening had been arranged
and she knew already what she would wear,
knew exactly what to say, knew how far
to walk into the dark along the water.
She'd click her beaded change purse closed
before she pushed open the door,
before we walked back uptown,
her bedroom slippers quiet on the sidewalk,
her small hands the color of moths
fluttering to a pause near the top
button of her flannel bathrobe.

Migraine

We could see it in our mother's walk,
a small unsteadiness, as if the house
gave way beneath her, and her eyes
drifted far back in her head,
almost not recognizing us,
her fingers rubbing her nose,
her temple, a wet cloth over an eye,
walking into a closet and staying there
for hours, her moaning worse, the pounding.
When she came out, she called Dr. Murray,
then told us she'd be right back,
to pull down the covers of her bed,
to watch for her in case the injection
took hold and knocked her out
before she made the three blocks
from the doctor's office, before
she crossed the street at Klinger's,
coal trucks rumbling down on her,
diesel horns blasting, air brakes hissing,
staggering back to us, barely able
to climb the stairs. My brother and I

took off her shoes, her hat,
her black coat, not knowing then
that what caused the headaches
was amino acids, and the sausages,
salami, and pickles she ate,
our house itself with its mine fumes
through a crack in the cellar floor,
my brother and I sitting on the back porch,
believing a neighbor man who called us
stupid, stupid Protestant kids
who caused our mother's headaches.
She would sleep fifteen hours,
then another hour sitting up in bed
until her eyes cleared,
until her mouth began to work again,
softly saying our names
and the names of all the streets in town,
finding her way back.

Deep Water Swimming Lesson

My daughter was next in line,
her pink suit brilliant and small,
a focus for all the things
I imagined could go wrong,
Joe Pizutti coming up all bloody
from the flooded mine hole we called the Molly,
the whole top of his skull
peeled back by a sharp rock.
And a friend who turned his back
a few seconds, and his small son
falling into the pond's deep end
without a sound, pulled out already blue.
I thought of rocks clicked underwater,
the cliff heating up in the afternoon.
We walked home along stripping roads,
afraid our parents would know we lied,
would smell the bottomless water all over us,
that our father waited at the crossing,
a switch in his hand, saying
dangerous, dangerous, and the switch
coming down against legs or across a back,

the pain remembered in the day's sharpness,
the sudden splash.

The Comet

Out of the blue my brother arrives
with his old baseball glove, and for the first time
in thirty years wants to throw a few.
And we do, over the length of my garden,
over peas, beans, habanaro peppers,
both of us throwing easy, warming up to it,
a curve that skids away, a knuckler,
both our hands stinging in the old way,
red when we take off our gloves and sit
on the grass, the evening coming on,
the sun slipping behind the hickory,
both of us talking about how neither saw
nor wanted to see the famous comet
when it came by that October morning,
vast and haunted, impossible to catch
the full curve of its coming and going,
thinking of our father showing us how
the heavens worked, using rubber balls,
hanging them from branches,
giving them a shove
so that they disappeared into the leaves,

then whirled back to us, both of us dodging them,
our father talking of time,
his white miner's face circling us, his eyes
drifting up into the sky above Girardville,
watching his pigeons, the clouds over the mountain,
the eyes that always came so easily back to us,
always swung the world up into the leaves
and brought it back down, holding us,
keeping us steady in those few feet of garden.

My Mother Ate Hill Dirt

Sometimes after rain, she walked
across the fields with her cloth bags and shovel,
to the hillside above the old orchard,
and dug down to where the clay mixed in,
then came back, bags over her shoulders,
red hair rising and falling. *A tonic,*
she said, as she emptied the bags
over the oilcloth on the kitchen table,
her fingers picking out grubs and stones.
Sometimes she baked it, sometimes
sprinkled it with vinegar and salt.
Once each year my father and I
tried some, gritty against our teeth,
chewy, a little sour. *No,* we said,
thank you, no, when she offered more.
By Easter the jars were empty,
washed and put on the top shelf
of an old cabinet in the middle cellar,
where years after her death I found them,
and almost didn't remember,
until I unscrewed a lid and held it close

to my face, the whole house filling again
with hillside and burlap bags, the way
I listened each night for those steps,
her bark-colored fingers brushing my hair,
goodnight, goodnight, those kisses
like slippery things just dug.

Yonko

I don't know if he could even talk,
that man who drove his cows
up or down Main Street, coal trucks and cars
in a line behind him. He had a stick
he used to keep the animals close
and he groaned after them, patting bony asses
or noses, wiping their drool over his pants.
We ran behind, yelling *Yonko, Yonko,*
crazy Yonko, throwing rocks at his cows,
laughing at the clumsy dance they'd do
when an udder was hit, or an ear.
He chased us, waving that stick,
his mouth purple and twisted,
his eyes wet and too close together.

We followed him past the Legion Memorial
with its cannon and rows of white crosses,
as far as the bridge at the end of town,
calling *Yonko, Yonko,* throwing a few last rocks,
though by then he was out of reach
and over the bridge to his shack
with its wire fence along the black creek.

We climbed the coal dirt banks,
then ran down them to the town dump,
piles of meat fat from the A & P,
shingles, plaster board, rusty nails,
seep of tomatoes, carrots, brown onions,
thick green puddles, tin cans
with their sharp lids peeled back,
ashes from all the stoves in town.
And bottles, hundreds of bottles,
that we smashed against bed frames,
bouncing them off blown-out tires
and wheelless baby carriages,
throwing gallon jugs into the air
and trying to shatter them with rocks,
not covering our faces when one exploded,
daring something all around us
that knocked on our doors each day.

Stealing Coal

We hopped it at the bottom
of the Ashland grade, caught a rung
of the steel ladder and swung up
over clanking and rattling couplings,
the bang of wheels over uneven rail joints.
Before we crossed the Homesville trestle,
we filled twenty burlap bags and pushed them off,
and another ten before the train began
to pick up speed on the Girardville flats.
Then down the ladder, pushing off
with a yell, hitting the ground running,
running as hard as we could,
running to keep from falling on our faces,
then slowing, in balance again, turning back
to what we could already hear cracking
in our mother's stove and the loaves turning brown—
that coal that took the three of us all day
to drag over the cinder banks
and down Zack's Hill to our house.

My Father's Hands

They brought him home, sleeves still smoking
from the flash fire in his mine, our mother's lips
a thin line of grief, Dr. Murray arriving
minutes later, peeling back skin from knuckles
and palms, greasing the wedding ring,
the Masonic ring with its red stone and diamond chip,
dropping it all to the floor, the injection
not helping my father at all, who groaned
and cursed the tunnels, the Welsh bosses.
He was home for months, his hands great wads
of cotton and tape that stank when we got too close,
trying not to let him know, trying not to imagine
what was under the bandages, that no longer fit anything,
all of us trying to avoid them the way we avoided
Skipper Todd who hiccoughed questions about our father
through a tube in his throat, none of us ever
saying more than our mother told us to say, never how
we'd suddenly awake and find them hovering over us,
never about how he'd sit for days in the coal cellar,
our mother feeding him down there, never about
the pounding that echoed up through the house
on Ash Alley, the house that began to fall down.

The Grand Canyon

Down into that staggering geography,
swallowed by it, knee ache and heel bruise,
the pack riding high as it's supposed to,
click of rock and gravel skid of boot.
It was a steady, relentless falling
past skunkbrush, manganite, lizards.
Three hours, six, the sliver of river
in view, then out. Plateaus, spires, ravens.
All of it shaped by the drip of water
and wind soft as the drape of a sleeve.
It was more than could be assembled
in a brain's lifetime, such angles and slashes.
He thought he'd come to the sepulcher's
absence and creak. At the river,
the walls went straight down
like blades into that red silt.
He could not even touch it. The bridge swayed
beneath him, its cables stretched.
He was deeper than his father had ever got
in his mine. He was digging to the end of it,
looking for petroglyphs, for one-armed Powell.

He was searching for a design.

The river sucked at him. Everything rose.

It was all a desert of distance and crumble.

He stayed one night, then another.

Rainbow trout slashed in the stream

past his camp. He wrote postcards.

A dark sky crackled and spun over the towers.

It was a narrow place.

It was like the neck of a bottle.

He wanted to go up a side canyon,

to find there in a stone basin of catchwater

a frog the size of his thumbnail,

its throat swollen with sobbing and trilling,

a frog that lived an afternoon,

a frog he'd listen to down to its last note.

Vultures

Three we found sheathed in ice
after a late freezing rain.
They were like glittering bottles
stuck on a branch,
their small eyes watching,
eyes that could see
rabbit guts half a mile away.
We lowered them in a sling
and carried them like logs to the shed.
Our daughter traced a finger
over the red turkey heads.
She lay next to them.
They were longer by inches.
Suddenly a horny leg broke through,
a shoulder, some wing feathers,
and then the stench of their true
design drove us away.
We left the shed door open and watched
from the kitchen as they wobbled out,
fussing their feathers, stretching their wings,
bouncing grotesquely, then rising easily,

beautifully, the world's real
pragmatists using the slightest updraft,
scanning the landscape, scouring it.
Their whole being was set for this
Puritan hatred of living flesh,
this love of neatness.

Fox

Last of the late snow along one edge
of the tree line that the fox crosses,
at first coming right at me,
one footstep into the next and the next,
all straightness and purpose, its red fur
puffed out, the white-tipped tail riding
on the level behind. What was on its mind
but mice or mole or finch too caught up
in thistle seed? The fox filled
to overflowing the chilly afternoon.
Suddenly, it barked, rose on its back legs,
and fell forward, breaking into a trot
toward the thick wild rose vines.
Long after it was gone, I knelt by its track,
and put my hand down flush over all of it,
those brilliant exhalations, sputterings,
splashes, the small cries across the field.

Deer

For nearly an hour in the early April dusk
I watched thirteen deer slowly feed
across winter wheat. You'd have thought
them part of the sky, so buoyant
they seemed, so delicately attached to earth,
black hooves hardly bending the wheat.
Every once in a while one would look
to where I knelt in a corner
of the L-shaped field, and stamp its foot,
ears nervous over the dark eyes
and the delicate lines of nose and neck,
or twitch its brilliant white tail.
Though I'd neither moved nor coughed,
something had drifted across the evening,
that took them, unhurried, toward the field's edge
and over its border of dry pennyroyal
and briars, into the woods, where one by one,
in that place, their shyness vanished
into the shyness among trees.

The Mink

Head level as a snake's, its body humped up
and richly brown, it came slithering
down the scree at broad noon.

It seemed a curl of smoke in and out
of the rocky shelves. Not a splash
as it poured itself into the stream.

Not a bubble to mark its underwater way.
Up on the rock again, a bluegill in its mouth,
it shook itself head to tail,

eating slowly, head and fins and bones.
It left nothing. The afternoon was all mint
and new honeysuckle as it fluffed

its lush endlessness,
then gone in a dazzle of pelt,
a flush of instinct, a coil of pure purpose.

Bear Jam

That summer along the park roads,
there were bear jams, clownish black bears
everywhere, standing upright like men
or rolling past on all fours like barrels in a river,
little pig eyes, noses afloat in the air
filled with exhaust and picnic baskets.
One man coated his little daughter's face
with something, honey or peanut butter,
and laughing, his daughter laughing
at the great bear lumbering toward them,
the father held the smeared girl
out before him, inviting the bear to lick,
the bear pigeon-toed, spoiled rotten by handouts,
closing in, its back high as the father's belt,
its tongue a sickly white as it covered
the girl's face, whose mouth was open,
who might have been screaming,
whose father laughed at his good fortune,
until the little girl tried to get away,
and the father tried to lift her back
and the bear took her between

his front paws like a doll and pulled.
It pulled and the father pulled.
We could see the claws deep against her t-shirt.
Her one shoe fell off. It took no more
than seconds in that day that was utterly clear,
so filled with spectacle and wilderness.
What true horror could have really been,
but the jaws never opened wider
than to let that thick tongue out,
and the paws that could kill a steer
with a single whack, suddenly let go,
simply fell away and padded casually off.

Two Beautiful Young Women

for Nancy and Betty

On a lustrous June day, they sit
on the grass next to the garden.
The air is smooth over their faces.
The easy wind ruffles hair and flax.
One is pregnant, her belly blue-veined
and taut beneath the white blouse.
The other, slender and green eyed,
names sorrel and sweet cicely,
the fairy trumpets of columbine.
A little marijuana smoke drifts off.
Each is beautiful. When they laugh,
the man stops hoeing his row of beans,
and looks at them. He sips his beer.
It is an afternoon like no other,
its portents everywhere against everything.
Earlier he'd sat with them, his hand
invited to that great, good belly.
It was all heavy and deep water.
Like the season, it was seeded and set,
snugged down for a few warm months.

My Wife Vanishes in a Field of Sunflowers

In this warm evening of cowbells
and cicadas, she kneels for a little while
by feverfew and lady's bedstraw,
then moves in an easy curve
past grapevines and zinnias,
and into the sunflowers,
the whole field closing around her.
She has taken off her sneakers and jeans,
hung panties and bra and blouse
on the wooden bench,
her arms flashing in and out
of the first few rows,
the giant heads trembling above her.
It is all I have of her for hours,
as I wait by the hickory,
imagining her spins, the spider webs
trailing across her face and shoulders,
her breath like good weather down the rows.

I grow nervous for her,
that she will lose the horizon

or vanish into one of the sinkholes,
or move into another field, and another,
or swirl like fog across the river.
I want to call out to her, but do not,
trusting as I do her instincts,
to keep this or that leaf in mind,
to remember the light as it unwinds
behind her like a thread.
I think of taking off my clothes
and following, of our small house
beneath the honey locusts,
the evenings of red wine and Vivaldi.
I watch for early constellations
whose names I do not know,
until at last at the corner of my eye
when I have been looking elsewhere,
there comes a paleness through the field,
as though something were rising
from a quiet pool by laurels,
and out of it she softly steps
and walks shyly toward me,

a sulphur butterfly in her hair,
a drift of pollen over shoulders and breasts,
and one leg scratched.
It could be relief or desire
that makes the evening catch in my throat,
it could be something in her face,
something that gathers as light does
along the edges of leaves in this season,
that does not startle the small bird
on its limb, that happens between us,
a small distance we have never named.

A Small Lovely Place

It is beebalm and calendula
you offer this bright morning,

before the sun heats fields almost to ignition,
and which blossom from your hand

as if you had suddenly remembered
a trick of ordinary air.

This red and yellow and blue,
this pale white of your fingers

slowly opening from around the stems,
hesitating a moment over them—

a cloud, a butterfly, a small lovely place
I will keep secret from all but the flowers.

Yellow Flowers

That crow on the wire outside my window,
something white under its horny foot,
part of a fish or a piece of crust.
It faces into the northeast wind
that came up overnight. Once I watched
a sharp-shinned hawk come fast
around the corner of my house,
then a puff of brown feathers.
The hawk landed beneath the blue spruce.
It took its time eating the sparrow.
Almost an hour, then some more
to clean its talons and beak against a branch.
Honed them, I would almost say,
like my father each morning
with his razor and strap, slowly back and forth,
that slippery sound like low water over rocks
that always caught some part of my mind,
balancing it perfectly as the crow
this morning over the small yellow flowers.

Beach Tent

Each day for a week we put it up,
tied a red handkerchief from one strut,
a white t-shirt from the other.
In the wind it thrummed and wanted
to fly off over the fishermen and children
at the edges of the waves.
We weighted each corner with sand,
not with sticks I used to snap from trees
to peg down the tent of my youth,
a carpet stretched over a clothesline,
the tent I slept in and heard crippled
Tony Picollo on his crutches
struggling drunk up his back steps,
his mother hissing at him in Italian.
Or my sister at dawn shushing me
as she sneaked into our house,
her boyfriend coasting his Indian
down Ash Alley before catching it in gear,
its roar and pound like the sea
twenty feet away, those few feet we splashed in
before the abyss began, that sunless place

of sullen, long-jawed faces with shrunken bodies,
that place the slime of life was thought to be,
that made the butterfly and marsh mallow,
the beautiful girls walking by,
all our sweet trouble at the edge of things.

The Bottomland

for Edward Humes, 1900–1962

Once each November I slide the Winchester
from its fleece-lined case, pull boots
and canvas hunting pants from the closet,
make a sandwich. My wife watches
but never once has asked why.
Nor have I ever said it's to see
my father walking again the ravine
where he fell that one season,
or that field where, not seeing me,
he shot at a ring-necked pheasant,
pellets stinging my back and legs.
Or that afternoon at the top of a draw
I saw something behind his face.
Or the way he kept the top button
of his hunting coat buttoned.

When I come to the spring
behind the empty stone farmhouse,
he's already there, eating a sandwich,
filling his collapsible tin cup.
We go into the rattling corn,

47

through the soybeans, along the stream.
We save the bottomland for last,
skunk cabbage and rotting logs.
It's where the dogs circle out of hearing
as we wait by the tree with its initials,
talking about my children, his mother,
my brother killed in a mine explosion,
how dry last summer was, the taste of fresh bread,
a few last things before it's time to leave.

The Last Day of August

All week hundreds of monarchs
rise above me as I walk
beneath the maples. Nights I go out
with a flashlight and touch wings,
a little powder coming off on my fingers.
And each morning still clustered there,
no birds swooping down at them,
not a cat or garter snake interested.
I think of you waking from a dream of Chagall
or walking the edge of the alfalfa,
and want to tell you what I have forgotten
in the long summer of children and water,
but remember again because of the butterflies,
and understand more clearly than ever
the shallow light drifting so delicately
over the leaves with their small holes,
and over the lawn chair with its long shadows,
the voices reaching us from the house
near the tree line. How much it all means,
this season ending so gently,
hardly a breath anywhere,

not even from all those wings
that early this morning before we woke
drifted south and left not a single trace.

Migration

The phoebe has stayed late
in the rose of Sharon,
fluttering down to snap moths
or butterflies out of the air.
In two days it will be autumn.
Already the ground is littered
with hickory nuts,
and the light sharper, and less.
The moon comes up behind the old orchard.
Purple drifts along the western edge
of the valley. On Hawk Mountain
the great migration of osprey
and peregrine settles
for the night in oak and pine.
A pale yellow has begun to rise
from the roots of the corn.

Dead Hawk

There it was, as yesterday and the day before,
still hugging its branch, one wing loose
and moving in the slightest wind.
Its head had wedged in a fork,
this red-tailed hawk, all whites and browns,
hollow boned, flight feathers still spread
against the blue April sky. It was a pile
of beauty settling against black bark,
all the stoops and pits and tendons,
the lush passageways of blood and vision
clotted and stopped, its talons still hooked
around some invisible prey. This predator
that could see a mouse from half a mile up,
that could hear wind over a rabbit's fur,
that had swooped after his mate through miles
of sky and flew belly-up beneath her.
All this now a frayed tracery of nothing at all.
I wanted to climb up to it and bring it down,
but the tree was wound around with poison,
the branches too snap-dry and far apart.
I did not want it to fall part by part,

covered with ants, stuck by crows and maggots.
I wanted to bring it down intact,
keeping only one tail feather, then dropping
the rest into the mine hole at the edge of the woods,
letting it fly one last time
toward the water that gurgled and fell far down.

My Daughter Wakes in the Fog

It is October.
It is before dawn.
The sleeping bag rises around her.
The wind is not yet in the pin oak and birch,
but something else rustles the branches
and dry snakeweed
beyond the tent flaps.
Outside, all is changed.
It is like looking through flannel.
She cannot see the fire ring.
She cannot see the next tent.
When she puts her hand out,
it comes back cool and slippery.
She watches swirls back and forth
over the camp,
and calls for us who are miles away,
the fog brushing our windows
and drifting over the porch with its pots
of purple asters and clusters of fallen leaves.
What can we know of such anguish?
We wake for no good reason,

thinking we hear her rustling in bed,
remembering she is not there.
She is somewhere else waiting for light,
for someone to find her.
There is nothing in the fog she recognizes.
She cries because she has never been so lonely
and, because her hands have lost hold of everything
except what is beneath her.
And this is how it is in the fog,
this hissing and dripping over leaves and branches,
this sitting still.

The Snow Boat

The night of the blizzard, our neighbor
stripped down to a pair of gray worsted trousers
and began circling his house and ours,
not making a sound, stopping once in a while
at our door for a glass of water,
a cookie, saying he could not come inside,
that he was looking for the snow boat
his father made him,
and off he'd go again into the storm,
his eyes bulging, his feet red,
little white spots on his fingers,
not seeming to mind any of it,
not our helplessness, not the absence
of his wife and children, his dog,
not the wind over the fields,
circling us well past midnight
until a jeep broke through the drifts,
our neighbor kneeling behind
a woodpile like someone about
to be patted or spanked,
oblivious to the shriek of wind,

breaking trees, torn-off shingles,
windows rattling, the snow sifting
under even the tightest door,
covering the places where he staggered and fell,
where he dug a tunnel down to the ground,
where he broke off a limb and made
paddle marks in the snow.

The Last Woods Bison, December 31, 1799

after Bil Gilbert

Because there was snow on the ground since Thanksgiving,
the herd was starving. Led by a bull called Old Logan,
they went into Middle Creek valley where they ate
a hay crop and trampled a woman and her baby.
It was cold. Sphagnum moss turned to crystals.
More snow drove over the seven ridges.
Their trail led into a steep-sided gorge
where the wind died a little, and animals
blacker than black powder rooted through ice for food.
The men found them there, first shooting them,
then going at them with bear knives and clubs.
It went on all afternoon, until the last one
was killed, but frozen in place did not fall.
Its tongue was cut out, and some of the others,
and roasted over a great fire.
In the dark the men marched back into the valley.
They sang hymns into the new century.

The Lime Kings

This February morning before dawn,
one of them is out there in his great truck
with its big balloon tires,
the stainless steel tank up high
behind the cab, outriggers let down on both sides
like spider legs, coils of tubes, valves,
and the pump sending out clouds
of lime dust over my neighbor's fields,
brilliant headlights coming in a line
along one edge, turning around, taillights
smaller and smaller, then across
the bridge to the other fields,
on and on in the gauze light beginning low
over the eastern hills. I think of my father
with his long-handled spade and bags of lime
on a Saturday in early March in his small patch.
Preparing it for the Resurrection,
he'd say, walking back and forth
until the half-dozen bags were empty
and his whole figure white from the hands back,
and then turning it under, and me sitting

on the concrete walk in my red
and black mackinaw, some of the lime
drifting to my face, bitter on my lips
so that I cried out and made a face,
my father stopping his work to wipe me off,
saying it was nothing but crushed chalk
like the stuff on the blackboard at school,
that it would make me grow,
raising his hand above my head,
saying, *This much by summer's end.*

Photograph of Three Young Women on a Spill Bank

for Doris McCaffrey Humes, 1900–1987

All are wearing white blouses,
long skirts, high leather shoes.
Two of them smile. One has long braids,
one has hair like evening clouds.
One wears a black headband.
You expect each of them to hold flowers.
Behind them, a mine engine and coal cars,
the colliery tipple with its cable and great wheels,
dullness of slag, piles of timber.
It might be Sunday, the mine idle.
A picnic, the young miners off to one side
playing baseball or talking of hounds and pigeons.
Each of the women would marry a miner.
Each would have children.
One husband would die slowly
in a caved-in tunnel even the rats had left.
He left a message scratched on his belt.
One, before he was thirty, would die
of a stroke caused by steady drink.
And the third, slowly running out of breath
in a miners' hospital, jumped from a window.

One of the women frowns, one turns slightly
to the left, and the one
in the middle stares straight ahead.
All the arms are bare from the elbow down,
the long white necks purposefully set.
Farther back you can see the ridge
all bumpy and cluttered with new laurel.
Seventy years ago, those smiles,
before it all came down,
before one of them began walking
ram-rod straight, back and forth, past
the doors of all the saloons on Second Street.
Before one grew lonely with her orchids
and African violets, the memorized Bible.
Before one of them each evening
went into a dirt cellar to cry and shriek.
All of them dead, the place where they stood
dug up or covered with birch and briars.
All of them alive, eyes steady
with the rest of the long afternoon,
their white blouses brimful of life.